Charlie –
Prince of
Wheels

Roy Apps

Illustrated by James Cottel

Contents

OXFORD
UNIVERSITY PRESS

The Case of the Talent Contest Crooks

Chapter 1

The best detective agency in town

I woke up to the sound of someone playing 'Jingle Bells'. Amazing! When I'd gone to bed it had been the beginning of November. Now, it was Christmas!

Then I remembered: 'Jingle Bells' was the new ring tone on my phone. I switched on the bedside lamp, leant over to pick up the phone and put it to my ear.

'Yeah? Aaaargh!'

A hot, sharp pain shot through my head. I removed the bedside lamp from my ear. Then I picked up the phone.

'Yeah?'

'Is that Charlie Chisholm?' stuttered an agitated voice.

Quickly, I looked at the cover of my English homework book, which was on my bedside table.

'Er, yeah. Who's that?'

'Alfie Buggins.'

I knew Alfie Buggins well. He was in my class at school. He was as thin as a broomstick and as daft as a brush. 'What do you want, Alfie?' I asked him.

'I want the best detective agency in town,' Alfie replied.

'Right,' I smiled. My exploits as Puddlethorpe-on-Sea's Toppermost Private Detective were well known.

'But I couldn't find their number,' Alfie went on, 'so I called you instead.'

I shot Alfie my coldest look. Then I remembered he was on the phone so he couldn't see me. 'OK then, Alfie,' I said. 'What gives?'

'Something really awful has happened! Can you come round?'

'What, now?'

'Yes! Unless you can get here sooner?'

I heard Alfie gulp. My private detective's brain told me that this could mean one of only two things: either he was very, very scared or he was drinking a can of cola. Either way, I knew that it wasn't good for a nervous nitwit of a nincompoop like Alfie Buggins to be left on his own if he was feeling scared.

'Is there anybody with you, Alfie?' I asked him.

'Just the one.'

'Just the one what?'

'Just the one body.'

I gasped. I gulped. I felt my hair beginning to stand on end – it always did that when I hung out of bed upside down.

'OK, Alfie,' I said. 'But before I come round to your place, I need one vital piece of information.'

'What's that?'

'Your address.'

Chapter 2
A matter of arrest

Alfie lived at 9 Tenby Gardens. I knew Tenby Gardens well – it was next to Elevenby Gardens.

I slid out of bed onto the seat of The Wheels. Then I realized I was still wearing my pyjamas, so I slipped on my clothes and then I moved back onto the seat of The Wheels. I flicked the ON switch, grabbed the joystick with my right hand and I was off. As I sped down the hall, I flicked another switch and the front door opened automatically. Then, as I hit the mean streets of Puddlethorpe-on-Sea, I thrust the joystick forward into full power. The Prince of Wheels was on the road!

lcome to Puddlethorpe-on-Sea

A word about The Wheels: cool. Another word about The Wheels: fast. The reason for this is all down to my mate, M. Her real name is Emily-Louise, but the only people who call her that are teachers or kids who don't know what's good for them!

M's brother works at Dipstick's Garage, developing a new state-of-the-art electric sports car. M goes down to the garage to give him a hand, and when she's not doing that, she practises on The Wheels. She's fixed The Wheels up with a 4-pole induction motor, a state-of-the-art multi-speed transmission and a tomato ketchup dispenser in the left arm rest; dead handy for when I pick up a bag of chips on the way home from school.

I zoomed across town at top speed and took the turning into Tenby Gardens on three wheels. There was a loud screech from my brakes as I arrived at Alfie's front door.

Then, there was a loud screech from Alfie as I parked on his foot.

'OK, where's the body?' I asked him.

Alfie nodded towards the hall. There, slumped on the floor with its head bent back, was a body. Its face was ugly and twisted. It was wearing old clothes and had a battered baseball hat on its head.

Alfie gave me a twisted kind of smile. 'I've made a pretty good job of him, don't you think, Charlie?'

A shiver of fear passed through me. I'd always thought that Alfie Buggins was like something that came out of a leaking tap, i.e. a great big drip. But there was no doubt about it: he was actually a callous, cruel, cold and calculating killer!

'I'm going to call the police,' I said.

'Why?' asked Alfie.

'It's a matter of arrest,' I replied, as calmly as I could.

'A rest?' retorted Alfie, crossly. 'I haven't got time for a rest. I've got things to do.' He waved his hand at the body. 'If I tied him onto the back of your wheels, could you tow him round to the bonfire in the back garden?'

'The bonfire?' I echoed in an appalled voice. 'You're going to burn him?'

'Of course!' Alfie said. 'What else do you do with a Guy Fawkes?'

There was a moment's silence as I tried to think of something to say. Then there was another moment's silence as I tried to think of something else to say.

Eventually I mumbled, 'Er … right. Yeah. Cool.' Then I remembered! 'Alfie, do you mean to say that you called me, Charlie Chisholm, Puddlethorpe-on-Sea's Toppermost Private Detective, round here just to help you put your Guy Fawkes onto the bonfire?'

'Of course not!' Alfie replied. 'I called you round here because I want you to help me find something I've lost, something that's very precious and important to me – '

'Alfie,' I interrupted him. 'Before you go any further, I must tell you that there's no way I can help you find your brain.'

'No, not my brain, Charlie! I've had something stolen – something I can't allow to fall into the wrong hands!'

'And what is it?' I asked.

Alfie looked up and down the street, his eyes wide with fear. 'I can't tell you,' he said. 'THEY might be listening!'

I didn't know who THEY were, but they were obviously big enough and scary enough for Alfie to be talking about them in CAPITAL LETTERS.

'OK,' I replied. 'Now let's get this Guy Fawkes out of here.'

Alfie hitched his Guy Fawkes on to the back of The Wheels and I towed it through the hall and into the kitchen. 'Right, Alfie,' I said sternly. 'Before I help you any more with this guy, you're going to tell me what precious thing of yours has been stolen.'

Alfie sighed, sadly. 'Well, it's like this – ' he began. But before he could get any further, the sound of violent hammering filled the air. Someone was trying to break down the kitchen door!

'Oooh!' Alfie whimpered. 'I knew it! It's THEM! They've come for me!'

He made a dash for the hall and tripped over the guy. As he grabbed the fridge door handle to try to break his fall, the fridge toppled over on top of him. Two dozen eggs broke over his head and a carton of milk leaked into his lap.

'Ooooooh!' Alfie cried. 'You're a genius, Alfie!' I told him. 'Disguising yourself as an omelette like that. They'll never find you now!'

The pounding at the kitchen door became louder and more insistent.

'Alfie Buggins, I know you're in there. Let me in!' growled the voice, menacingly.

I gasped, for it was a voice I recognized only too well.

Chapter 3
Bangers and Mash

I knew there was only one thing I could do to stop the dreadful hammering on the kitchen door.

'Er ... come in!' I called. 'It's not locked.'

The door burst open. There stood a glowering, towering figure, wearing a bright pink puffa jacket, camouflage trousers and a pair of size 8 army boots.

'Oh, hello M!' I said. 'What are you doing here?'

M scowled at me. 'You texted me, bozo!' She took out her phone and read the screen: *Gut round 2 9 10by girdons quack!*'

'I was getting dressed at the time,' I explained. 'It's not easy texting while you've got your pyjama top around your head.'

'What's she doing here?' muttered Alfie, with a pout.

'If you want me to solve your robbery,' I told him, sharply, 'M is part of the deal; she's like my sidekick.'

'What does that mean?' asked Alfie.

'If Charlie does something stupid, I kick him in the side,' M explained. 'OK, Alfie, spill the beans.'

'Must I?' whined Alfie. 'I've already spilt the eggs and the milk.'

'What M means,' I explained, 'is that we need to know what it is that's been stolen. It's not your games console, is it?'

Alfie shook his head. 'No, it's worse than that!'

'Your phone?' asked M.

Alfie shook his head again. 'No, it's even worse than that!' He paused. 'They've stolen my award!'

'Your award?' I repeated, flabbergasted. I couldn't imagine anyone giving Alfie an award, unless it was for Pea-brain of the Year.

'Yes,' Alfie went on. 'My award as winner of this year's Puddlethorpe's Got Talent contest.'

'That's amazing!' I said.

'You're telling me,' snorted M. 'The Puddlethorpe's Got Talent contest doesn't start until six o'clock this evening. How come you've already won it?'

'There are only two singers in the contest and I'm a zillion times better than the other one,' Alfie declared, rather grandly. 'But now the award that is rightfully mine has been cruelly snatched from me!'

'Explain yourself,' snapped M.

'It's like this,' said Alfie. 'Once upon a time, I used to be a Little Weed.'

'I didn't realize you'd ever stopped,' I muttered.

'I mean,' Alfie went on, 'when I was about three, I used to go to the Little Weeds Nursery. It was really nice – there was a wooden train set where I could play choo-choos and a model farm where I could play moo-moos.'

'Alfie,' growled M. 'Just get on with it!'

'We sang lots of jolly songs and the nursery teacher made a recording of me singing one of them. It was called "I'm a Little Buttercup". A few weeks ago I saw that it had been posted online. As soon as I realized, I had it taken down, but not before somebody had made a DVD of it – somebody who doesn't want me to win Puddlethorpe's Got Talent!'

'And who would that be?' I asked.

'Ed Banger,' sighed Alfie.

I might have known. Ed Banger was in our class at school, and together with his mate,

Mo Mash, he ran the dreaded Bangers and Mash gang.

'Ed's in charge of the sound system at Puddlethorpe's Got Talent,' Alfie explained. 'A sound system that includes a DVD player. When I come onto the stage, he's going to switch on the DVD player and I'll be up there on the big screen, singing "I'm a Little Buttercup". Then everyone will laugh at me and I'll be too embarrassed to perform, and the Puddlethorpe's Got Talent Award will go to the other person in the contest.'

'And who is this other person?' asked M.

'Felicity Foggorn!' wailed Alfie.

I gasped. Felicity Foggorn was Ed Banger's ghastly and gruesome girlfriend.

Alfie wiped away a dollop of egg yolk from his cheek. 'While you two go and get the DVD back, I think I'll go and change out of this omelette,' he said.

Chapter 4

Pit stop

M put the Guy Fawkes up on a kitchen chair, out of the way. Then she leapt onto the little platform at the back of The Wheels and I thrust the joystick forward. I suppose it would've been better if I'd opened the kitchen door before we charged through it, but when M and I are hot on a case, nothing gets in our way!

We sped along the mean streets until we reached Puddlethorpe School, where Puddlethorpe's Got Talent was being held. We screeched across the playground and came to a halt next to the hall.

'Right M, are you ready? Let's head straight in and grab that DVD,' I said.

We peered through the windows. Ed, Mo and the rest of the Bangers and Mash gang were setting up the sound equipment on the stage. I gulped. They looked big, they looked bulky and they looked very, very sulky. They had scowls on their faces that would have scared off a pack of Rottweilers.

'Er ... on the other hand, I suppose we could just sneak off,' I suggested.

'You're right, Charlie,' agreed M. 'If we go in there, we'll end up getting our noses biffed, our ears boxed and our heads battered.'

'But if we go straight back to Alfie's place and tell him we were too scared of the Bangers and Mash gang to get the DVD back, we'll look like a right couple of bozos,' I pointed out.

M nodded. 'Tell you what, let's go down to the garage. You can work out a plan while I give The Wheels a once over.'

While M turned her hand to tuning up The Wheels, I turned my brilliant brain to the problem of how to get the DVD back from Ed Banger without getting our heads bashed in.

Eventually, M put her spanners and screwdrivers away. 'I've adjusted the spiral bevel pivot gear to give you more torque.'

'Er, brilliant, M!' I said. Though I hadn't the faintest idea what she was wittering on about.

'I've also refined the aerodynamic styling on the front wheel arches,' M went on.

'Yeah?' I replied, hazily.

M groaned. 'You don't know what I'm talking about, do you?'

'Er ... not exactly,' I admitted.

'Where The Wheels got bent when you smashed through Alfie's kitchen door? I've knocked them all out with a hammer,' M explained.

'Thanks M. That's great!' I said.

'I've also fixed you up with a two-tone horn.'

I pressed the button M had fixed on the side of the arm rest.

'PARPPPP!'

It was so loud, it rattled my teeth. It rattled my tongue and my tonsils as well.

'Where did you get this from? A twenty tonne articulated lorry?'

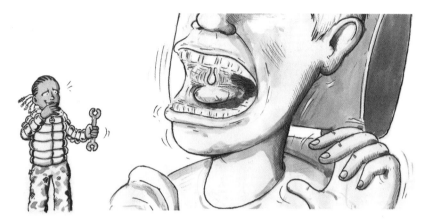

M shook her head. 'From a forty tonne articulated lorry. So, what's your idea for getting that DVD back from Ed Banger?'

'Er ... I haven't got one.'

M sighed. 'Then we'll just have to drive back to Alfie's – very, very slowly.'

We found Alfie in the street outside his house, trying to hide behind a lamp-post.

'Oooh, I'm so scared,' Alfie wailed. 'They've broken into the house!'

I frowned. 'But we've just seen Ed Banger and his gang; they're all at the school.'

Alfie led us round the back of the house. 'Then tell me who else would have done this,' he demanded, with a quiver in his voice. 'The vicious and violent villains have smashed the kitchen door down!'

'Ah,' I said.

'Ah,' M said.

'Still, they can't hurt me now,' Alfie muttered.

'What do you mean?' I asked him.

'Not now you've got the DVD back,' Alfie replied.

'Oh yes, your DVD,' M said, giving me one of her most infuriating smiles. 'Charlie was just going to explain about that.'

Chapter 5
A stroke of luck

Alfie was fuming. Alfie was furious. Not only that, he was also very cross indeed.

'Call yourself the Prince of Wheels?' he yelled at me. 'You're more like the Prince of Wallies!' He started to stomp towards the kitchen door. Then, all of a sudden, he stopped. His hair stood on end. His *ears* stood on end.

'Aaaargh!' he screamed.

We raced over to see what had scared him. There, at the kitchen table, sat Alfie's Guy Fawkes.

I have to admit, it did look rather gruesome. Not quite as gruesome as Alfie, standing there with his hair and ears all sticking up, but gruesome enough. Suddenly, my brilliant brain came up with a blistering idea.

'Got it!' I yelled. 'We need the dummy!'

'Well, you're not having me!' wailed Alfie.

'Not you, Alfie – your Guy Fawkes! I've just worked out how we can get that DVD back!'

I grabbed the guy as M leapt onto the back of The Wheels. Once again we headed for Puddlethorpe School hall. We zoomed past three sports cars, two motorbikes and a police car. OK, so they were parked at the kerb, but it still felt good.

Ed Banger and his gang were still busy setting up the sound system. M crept in through the back door and carefully placed Alfie's guy on one of the seats in the back row. Then, bending down so she couldn't be seen, she chanted, 'Ed Banger is a der-brain! Mo Mash is one, too!'

Then she raced out to join me in the playground. We peered into the hall to see Ed Banger, Mo Mash and their gang charging down the hall. They grabbed the guy.

'Who are you calling der-brain, der-brain?' snarled Ed, giving the guy a biff.

'Yeah, who are you calling der-brain, der-brain?' growled Mo, giving the guy a bash.

The rest of the gang set to biffing and bashing the guy and shouting and yelling as well.

Suddenly, from the stage, there came a deafening cry, 'Ed, Mo and the rest of you boys, what do you think you're doing?'

It was Miss Angel, our class teacher, who was organizing Puddlethorpe's Got Talent. 'You obviously cannot be trusted to behave yourselves. Leave the hall immediately! All of you!'

M and I hid as Ed, Mo and the rest of the gang skulked away across the playground. I gave The Wheels a thump in delight. Unfortunately, the bit of The Wheels I thumped in delight was the new two-tone horn M had fixed up for me.

'PARPPPP!'

'Charlie, you bozo!' hissed M; as Ed, Mo and the rest of the Bangers and Mash gang spun round and saw us.

'We'll get you, Charlie Chisholm!' roared Ed. 'You and your silly girlfriend!'

Ed, Mo and the rest of them started moving menacingly towards us.

'Quick, Charlie!' urged M.

In a flash, we had nipped through the doors and into the hall.

'Hello, Miss!' called M.

Miss Angel greeted us with a smile. 'Emily-Louise! Charlie!' she beamed. 'What a stroke of luck! I need a couple of volunteers to operate the sound system for tonight's Puddlethorpe's Got Talent contest. Would you be able to help, do you think?'

'No problem, Miss!' replied M, giving me a knowing wink.

Chapter 6
Horrible and hilarious!

As soon as we got our hands on the sound system, M grabbed the DVD and zipped it up tight in the pocket of her jacket.

That evening, at Puddlethorpe's Got Talent, Alfie sang 'Circle of Life' from *The Lion King*. Unfortunately, he'd brought the wrong backing track with him, so he had to sing it to the tune of 'The Wheels on the Bus'. I don't think people noticed too much. Both songs are about things that go round, after all.

Anyway, Alfie was loads better than Felicity Foggorn. She didn't get any marks at all – mainly because none of the judges heard her sing. They'd all put their fingers in their ears as soon as she opened her mouth.

After the show, I dropped M off at her place.

'So that's another case sorted by the Prince of Wheels and his trusty sidekick,' she said with a smile.

I nodded.

'You don't look so happy about it,' M said.

I shrugged. 'It's just that, well ... I know we sorted the case but, now that Alfie's got the DVD back, it means we'll never get a chance to have a really good laugh at him singing "I'm a Little Buttercup".'

M gave me a sly grin. 'Who said Alfie had got the DVD back?'

She put her hand inside her jacket and pulled out Alfie's DVD.

Five minutes later, we were in M's sitting room and up on the plasma screen came a picture of a very little Alfie Buggins with a very large buttercup chain dangling round his neck. He gave a soppy smile, opened his mouth and croaked in a squeaky voice:

'I'm a little buttercup
The prettiest of the bunch
But when the cows come in the field
They eat me for their lunch.'

It was horrendous, it was horrible. And ... it was absolutely hilarious!

The next night was the 5th of November. M and I motored over to Alfie's to watch the fireworks. We found him with the other guests, putting the finishing touches to the bonfire.

'Glad you could come,' Alfie said to us. 'And thanks for giving me the chance to win Puddlethorpe's Got Talent.'

'No problem,' I said.

M pulled the DVD out of her pocket and handed it to Alfie.

'I think you'd better destroy this,' she said, 'before it causes any more trouble.'

'Right,' said Alfie, with a nod.

He took the DVD and, making sure no one was looking, slipped it into the pocket of the Guy Fawkes. Then we stood back while the bonfire was lit. The flames began to leap up into the sky; soon the guy and the DVD would be no more.

Suddenly, Alfie clapped his hands. 'And now,' he announced to all the guests, 'I'd like to sing the song that won me Puddlethorpe's Got Talent, "Circle of Life" from *The Lion King*!'

'Quick, Charlie, start the motor!' M hissed in my ear.

By the time Alfie had hit – or more likely missed – his first note, M and I were already on The Wheels, speeding away along Tenby Gardens and off towards the bright lights of downtown Puddlethorpe-on-Sea.

The Case of the Chocolate Cheesecake Cheats

Chapter 1
Ned Rose Day

'Today,' Mr O'Dreary, our head teacher, announced, 'we have a very important guest in assembly – the chairman of the school governors, Councillor Ned Rose!'

Councillor Ned Rose stood up. His bald head shone so brightly that he could have starred in an advert for furniture polish. 'I've got a brain-teaser for you all,' he beamed. 'I wonder if anybody can guess what Tuesday is?'

Honestly, what a dumb question. I touched the calendar tab on my phone, and saw that Tuesday was the 18th of June. I was about to put my hand up when Alfie Buggins called out, 'The day between Onesday and Threesday?'

Councillor Ned Rose's left eyebrow twitched and he quickly went on, 'It's my birthday! So I have decided it should be called Ned Rose Day, after me. To celebrate this very special day, I'm inviting everyone at Puddlethorpe School to get themselves into teams and raise money for a charity of their choice. I will personally double the sum raised by the most successful team!'

This had to be the most exciting thing to have happened at Puddlethorpe School since Mr O'Dreary got stuck on the kitchen roof while trying to rescue Year 1's Jolly Giant art project.

Just about everyone in our class volunteered to do something for Ned Rose Day: Lily Gumboyle offered to charge people for a ride on her pony, Tony; Jamie Dodger offered to charge people to shake the paws of his puppy, Jaws; and Desi Desai offered to charge people for a stroke of his pet snake, Jake.

M and I decided that I would do a sponsored race around the school playground in The Wheels. The more laps I could do in fifteen minutes, the more money we'd raise for the charity of our choice, which was the Puddlethorpe Oldies' Wrestling Club – or POW! for short. M's granny was their secretary.

In fact, the only people who weren't doing anything were Ed Banger and Mo Mash.

'Raising money for charity? I'd rather spend the afternoon eating frog spawn,' had been Ed's comment.

'I'd give everything to charity to watch Ed eat frog spawn,' I'd offered.

Miss Angel, our class teacher, had told me to be quiet and carry on with my painting of Boudicca carving up Roman soldiers with her fiendish chariot wheels. Oh well, at least with the Bangers and Mash gang out of the way, Ned Rose Day was guaranteed to be trouble free.

Or so we thought.

On the Monday before Ned Rose Day, Ed put his hand up in class. 'Please, Miss Angel,' he said. 'Me and Mo would like to take part in Ned Rose Day.'

Everyone gasped, apart from Miss Angel – she gulped. 'Er ... what are you thinking of doing?' she asked Ed. There was a note of panic in her voice.

'We thought we'd bring in our home-made chocolate cheesecakes to sell,' Ed replied, sweetly.

Miss Angel looked relieved. 'That's nice!' she said. 'And what will you be collecting for?'

'SOBAMG!' declared Ed.

'And what's SOBAMG?' asked Miss Angel.

'Er ... Save Our Baboons, Apes, Monkeys and Gorillas,' explained Mo. 'They're endangered species. We saw a documentary last night about it. There are baby baboons out there in the jungle who are friendless and motherless – it's so sad.'

He was right. Lily Gumboyle was already in tears. 'Poor, poor baby baboons,' she sobbed.

'Don't worry, Lily,' said Mo. 'You can help the baboons by giving us loads of money tomorrow!'

There was no doubt about it, Ed and Mo were up to something. The question was, what?

Chapter 2

Danger at Dodgers

M and I cruised down to Dipstick's Garage, where she fine-tuned the motor on The Wheels, ready for my Ned Rose Day sponsored race.

When she'd finished, she said, 'You know we were learning about the Romans the other day? Well, I've got a really great idea for another accessory for The Wheels. Remember those swords Boudicca had sticking out of her chariot?'

'You got swords? Cool!' I yelled, excitedly.

'Actually, I haven't got any swords,' M explained. 'But I do have this.' She held up a snooker cue. 'I'll cut it in half. The two bits will slip inside your rear axle easily with one in each end.'

She was right. She fixed up a switch on my arm rest and when I pressed it, the snooker cues shot out of my rear wheel axle. It was brilliant!

'That is so cool, M!' I exclaimed. 'Er ... what do I use them for?'

'I don't know,' muttered M. 'Do I have to think of everything? Anyway, I fancy a bite of something to eat and you're paying.'

As we motored along the mean streets of Puddlethorpe-on-Sea, I shouted over my shoulder to M, 'I think there's something fishy about Ed Banger.'

'Yes,' M agreed. 'His face does look rather like a stuffed trout.'

'It's just that I can't imagine him baking home-made cheesecakes to sell for charity,' I said.

'Eeeeee ...' There was a screech from the brakes as I executed a near-perfect 360 degree handbrake skid outside Dodger's Delicious Deli and Bakery.

'Eeeeee!' There was a screech from M as she was thrown forward.

'Eeeeee!' There was another screech from M as she bashed her front teeth on my headrest. 'Bozo!' she yelled. 'When I said I fancied a bite

of something to eat, a nice leathery chunk
of your headrest wasn't what I had in mind!'

Honestly, there's no pleasing some people.
'Sorry, M,' I said. 'I'll treat you to one of
Dodger's Custard and Mustard Muffins.'

I was already at the door. I turned the handle
and pushed, but nothing happened.

'Maybe they're closed,' suggested M.

'What makes you think that?' I asked.

'The sign in the window that says CLOSED?'

'But it's mid-afternoon!' I protested. 'They're
always open at this time of day.'

'Yes ... ' agreed M, thoughtfully. 'There's
something about this situation, Charlie, that
reminds me of Alfie Buggins' haircut.'

'What do you mean, M?'

'I mean it's very strange. Come on, let's go
round the back and investigate.'

The back door to the bakery swung creakily
on a pair of rusting hinges and we went in. It
was dismal, dark and dreary. It was also very
eerie. In fact, it was so eerie that my whole body

shook like a bowl of sloppy custard and my knees quivered like a plate of jelly. Yes, there was no doubt about it, I was turning into a trifle.

Suddenly, M let out a dreadful scream. In the darkness, I could just see that her head was being held in a vice-like grip. Her assailant stood behind her, brandishing a long, thick white stick above his head.

'Don't move,' he growled at me, menacingly, 'or your girlfriend gets it!'

'She's not my girlfriend!' I protested. 'She's my mechanic!'

Chapter 3

A bit of a jam

I could just make out the light switch at the side of the door. I flicked it on to reveal the most horrifying sight. A trail of red, sticky mess was spread all the way across the bakery floor. The walls dripped and oozed the same terrible, blood-red liquid.

My eyes turned to look at M's attacker. With a shock, I realized that he was none other than Jamie Dodger, from our class at school! It was his family who ran Dodger's Delicious Deli and Bakery.

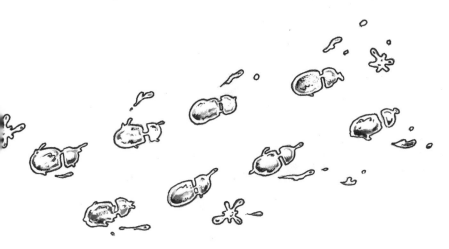

'Jamie,' I sighed. 'Why are you grabbing M round the neck and holding that baguette over her head?'

'Charlie?' he gasped in surprise. Then he turned to look at M. 'And M?' he said with a frown. 'I didn't recognize you. Your face seems to have changed.'

'I had a slight argument with the back of Charlie's headrest,' muttered M, scowling at me.

'OK, Jamie,' I ordered. 'Nice and slowly now, drop the baguette!'

'Why?' asked Jamie. 'Are you hungry?'

'Yes I am, actually,' I replied. 'You haven't got a large Custard and Mustard Muffin by any chance, have you?'

'Charlie,' said M, firmly, 'don't you think there's something else you should be asking Jamie?'

'Sorry, M.' I looked sternly at Jamie. 'You haven't got *two* large Custard and Mustard Muffins by any chance, have you?'

'I meant,' snapped M, 'the sticky mess across the floor and the red stains on your shirt and trousers – it looks like blood to me.'

'I know!' said Jamie.

'What happened, Jamie?' I asked.

'I'd just come home from school,' he explained, 'when I noticed the back door to the bakery was open. When I went in to investigate, I saw that there were two gruesome looking guys in here. They saw me and started to attack me!'

'Were they armed?' M enquired.

Jamie nodded.

'What, with baguettes?' I asked.

Jamie shook his head. 'No, worse than that – they were armed with jam doughnuts!'

I was amazed! I was astonished! I was astounded, too. 'What! Do you mean to say that the red sticky stuff smeared across the floor and walls, and all down your shirt and trousers, isn't blood?'

'Blood? Of course it isn't blood – it's strawberry jam!' Jamie replied.

'Mmm ... Yummee-e-e!' I declared, putting my finger in one of the biggest splodges on the wall and having a good lick.

Jamie caught his breath. 'Er ... actually, when I said it's strawberry jam, I didn't mean it's *all* strawberry jam.'

'What! Are you saying that the stuff I've just licked off my finger isn't strawberry jam?' Suddenly, I felt sick – very sick indeed.

Jamie shook his head. 'Honestly, Charlie,' he

snorted. 'Of course the dollop you've just licked off your fingers isn't strawberry jam, it's *raspberry* jam! Can't you tell the difference between strawberry jam and raspberry jam?'

'Of course I can!' I retorted crossly. 'What is giving me trouble, though, is telling the difference between you and a brainless bozo!'

'So when Charlie and I came in just now,' M asked Jamie, 'you thought the guys had come back, and that's why you attacked me?'

Suddenly, Jamie looked really worried. 'I don't

have to answer your questions!' he snapped angrily.

'But we could help you find out who the intruders were!' M protested.

'Yes,' I said. 'M and I are Puddlethorpe-on-Sea's Toppermost Private Detective Duo!'

'Didn't you hear what I said?' Jamie shouted. 'I don't want you two snooping around!'

Suddenly, from further inside the bakery, there came the sound of a hideous howling.

'Goodness! What's that?' M asked in alarm.

'That's Jaws, my Rottweiler puppy,' snarled Jamie. 'Now go away before I set him on to you!'

And, waving the baguette wildly above his head, he chased us both out of the bakery.

Chapter 4

The penny drops

M and I sat in the kitchen at my place, tucking into a plate of banana and tomato ketchup sandwiches.

M looked me straight in the eye and asked, 'OK, Charlie, what do you think?'

'Not bad,' I replied.

'What do you mean, "not bad"?'

'These banana and tomato ketchup sandwiches, they're not bad.'

'I meant what do you think about what we've just seen at Dodger's Bakery, bozo,' replied M crossly. She had a point. It was the point of the tomato ketchup bottle and she was aiming it at my nose. 'Why didn't Jamie want us ... er, what were his words?'

'Hang on a moment, I'll just go back to page 48 to check,' I replied. 'Ah yes, he said, he didn't want us "snooping around".'

'I think he's got something to hide,' said M.

I handed M my phone. 'Have a look at these photos,' I told her. 'I took them when Jamie wasn't looking. Now, what can you see?'

'A shelf labelled Perfect Pastries which is full of pastries, a shelf labelled Brilliant Buns which is full of buns and a shelf labelled Choicest Chocolate Cheesecakes which is ... empty!'

'Exactly!' I agreed. 'The burglars stole some chocolate cheesecakes. Even more reason, you would've thought, for Jamie to want our help.'

'But supposing he allowed the burglars to take the cheesecakes and then helped them throw jam doughnuts all over the place to make it look as if he'd put up a fight. And another thing: Jaws, his Rottweiler puppy! Why didn't he set Jaws on them ... Unless he was in on the theft with the burglars? No wonder he didn't want our help!'

'But who would want a whole shelf full of chocolate cheesecakes?' I frowned.

Then, suddenly, the penny dropped; I picked it up. 'Oh no ... Ed Banger! He and Mo are selling home-made chocolate cheesecakes at Ned Rose Day tomorrow!'

M snorted. 'I knew there was something fishy about Ed's idea! "Home-made" chocolate cheesecakes, indeed! Those cheesecakes will all have been stolen from Dodger's Bakery!'

There was no doubt about it, M was really excited. All her sentences were ending in exclamation marks!

But I was still puzzled. 'Why did Jamie let Ed and Mo take all the cheesecakes?'

'Perhaps Ed and Mo are paying him for them?' suggested M.

'But they're not making any money from Ned Rose Day,' I said. 'The money is all going to their endangered species charity.'

M sighed. 'Those two are up to something,' she said. 'What it is exactly, I don't know. But the whole business has all the hallmarks of my dad's aftershave – in other words, it stinks.'

Chapter 5
Miserable meanies

The Ned Rose Day fund-raising activities weren't taking place until the afternoon, so during the morning we had normal, boring lessons. In Maths, we all had to work on our tables – six of the class had fallen off them. In English, we'd had a rilly treacky spilleng tost.

I kept sneaking looks at Ed and Mo. They both looked as smug as ever. Jamie was hiding away at the back of the class, keeping his head down. It was all very suspicious.

During morning break, Mo and Ed came up to me. Mo put his face close to mine. I could see the bits of wood between his teeth where he'd been biting the ends of pencils.

'A friendly word of warning, Chisholm,' he snarled. 'Stay out of our way this afternoon or we'll ... er ...' He turned to Ed. 'What will we do, Ed?'

'Let all the air out of his tyres,' growled Ed.

'Oh yeah? Well, I've got a friendly warning for you,' I said. 'Stay out of our way this afternoon or we'll ... er ...' I turned to M. 'What will we do, M?'

'Let all the air out of his brain,' growled M.

M and I spent lunchtime out in the playground where she made some last minute checks to The Wheels.

'We can't let them get away with it,' she grumbled, angrily. We could see Ed and Mo through the hall windows, setting up their chocolate cheesecake stand.

'Get away with what?' I asked. 'Ed's only crime is that he hasn't baked those chocolate cheesecakes himself. And no one's going to worry about that if he raises lots of money for Save Our ... whatever it is.'

'Baboons, Apes, Monkeys and Gorillas,' muttered M, reading the big banner that Mo was busily putting up above the cake stand. Suddenly, she gasped. 'Why, of all the miserable and miserly meanies! Take another look at the letters on that banner, Charlie! SOBAMG could stand for Save Our Baboons, Apes, Monkeys and Gorillas, I suppose. But on the other hand, it could be 'Save Our Bangers And Mash Gang!'

'Of course!' I declared.

'All we need now is the proof,' said M.

'That's not difficult,' I replied. 'Come on! We've got to get to Mrs Office in the nurdle, quick! I mean, we've got to get to Mrs Nurdle in the office, quick! We can check if they really did see a TV documentary about baby baboons.'

As I thrust the gearstick forward, M leapt

onto the back of The Wheels. We headed across the playground, hurtled through the door, dashed along the corridor and crashed into the school office.

'Emily-Louise! Charlie! It's usually considered good manners to knock before you come into the school office!' said Mrs Nurdle sternly.

'Sorry, Mrs Nurdle,' said M. 'We'll knock when we go out instead.'

'Can we borrow your computer, please, Mrs Nurdle?' I asked.

Mrs Nurdle frowned. 'What for?'

'We want to see what was on TV last Sunday night,' explained M.

'*Doctor Who*?' suggested Mrs Nurdle.

'The only person in this school who'll need a doctor will be Ed Banger,' I retorted.

Mrs Nurdle raised her eyebrows. 'Ah, it's like that, is it,' she said, knowingly. 'I thought he might be up to his old tricks again. He and Mo have been looking dreadfully pleased with themselves recently – and that always means trouble.' She moved out of the way so that we could get to her computer.

We scanned the listings for Sunday for every TV channel, but none of them had screened a wildlife documentary about baboons. Then M typed SOBAMG into the browser. It drew a blank.

'There's no such charity as Save Our Baboons, Apes, Monkeys and Gorillas,' I muttered.

'Did you really think there would be?' replied M. 'They're going to keep the money they raise from selling Dodger's chocolate cheesecakes for themselves, after giving Jamie his cut, of course.'

'What do we do now?' I asked M, when we had left the office. 'We've got all the proof we need.'

'Right now, we can't do anything,' M replied. 'You're taking part in a sponsored wheelchair race around the playground, remember?'

The Wheels did M and I proud. I managed forty-two and a half laps in fifteen minutes. We'd raised a good sum of money for Puddlethorpe Oldies' Wrestling Club.

Other people did well, too. Desi Desai had a queue of Year 1s wanting to stroke his pet snake, Jake. Nobody wanted to shake the paws of Jamie's Rottweiler puppy, Jaws, though.

I looked across at Ed and Mo. They had collected loads of money and looked more smug than ever.

'Right, Charlie. Let's expose those two for the cheats that they are,' muttered M. 'If they try to make a dash for it, get ready to chase after them in The Wheels.'

I nodded. 'Don't you worry, M. I won't let them get away.'

Chapter 6
What a shot!

Everyone had gathered in the hall for Councillor Ned Rose's speech.

'And the team which has raised the most during Ned Rose Day is ... Ed Banger and Mo Mash!' declared Councillor Ned Rose. 'So, as promised, I will double the sum they've raised for Save Our Baboons, Apes, Monkeys and Gorillas.'

As Mr O'Dreary started to lead the applause, I sounded the horn on The Wheels. Everyone turned to stare at M and me.

'One moment,' I said. 'Ed and Mo claim they've been moved to raise money for endangered species because of a wildlife documentary they'd seen on the TV. M and I have checked the TV listings. There was no wildlife documentary on any TV channel on Sunday night.'

Now everyone turned to stare at Ed and Mo.

'Er ... it might have been Saturday night?' stuttered Mo, nervously.

M stood up. She shook her head. 'A quick check of the Internet shows that there is no wildlife charity called Save Our Baboons, Apes, Monkeys and Gorillas, or SOBAMG. Which is hardly surprising really, because SOBAMG doesn't stand for Save Our Baboons, Apes, Monkeys and Gorillas; it stands for Save Our Bangers And Mash Gang! Ed and Mo have raised all this money for themselves! And they got the chocolate cheesecakes from Jamie Dodger who is in on the scam!'

The hall exploded in an uproar.

I got ready to fire up The Wheels. As I glanced down, I saw to my horror that the LOW BATTERY warning light was flashing! Racing forty-two and a half laps around the playground had left me with hardly any charge in the motor!

I began to inch The Wheels out of the hall. The motor was so slow, I was hardly moving. I managed to get halfway across the playground, hoping to make it to the other side and block the school gateway. But by now, I had almost ground to a halt.

I turned round and saw that Ed and Mo had legged it through the hall doors and were racing across the playground towards me. If they managed to get past me, they'd be away and out of the school before anyone could stop them.

'You won't catch us, Chisholm,' Ed shouted. He and Mo were now almost level with The Wheels. 'Your battery's flat!'

I hit the switch on the arm rest and the two bits of my Queen Boudicca Snooker Cue shot out of each end of the axle. With a wild cry, Ed tripped over the right one and then Mo tripped over the left one. They both crashed to the ground.

'Maybe – but it's not as flat as you are, Ed Banger,' I replied with a grin.

Chapter 7
Something different

Once everybody had calmed down, Miss Angel
sorted things out. The money Ed and Mo had
raised was divided up between all the other
charities. When she told Jamie Dodger's mum
and dad that Jamie had let Ed and Mo steal all
their chocolate cheesecakes, they were furious.
They told him he'd have to stay in for four whole
Saturdays baking extra cheesecakes to make up
for it.

M's gran was pleased with the money we'd raised for Puddlethorpe Oldies' Wrestling Club. Now they'd be able to buy proper leotards to wear when they were wrestling.

After school, M and I went back to my place.

'Another successful case for Puddlethorpe-on-Sea's Toppermost Private Detective Duo,' I said.

'Mmm,' agreed M. 'Do you know what all this hard work catching the Bangers and Mash gang makes me feel, Charlie?'

'Proud?' I suggested.

'Hungry,' replied M.

'I'll make us some banana and tomato ketchup sandwiches,' I said.

'Charlie?' M asked.

'What?'

'We always have banana and tomato ketchup sandwiches. Can't we have something completely different?'

'Like what?'

'How about pineapple and tomato ketchup sandwiches?'

The Case of the Father Christmas Fraudsters

Chapter 1

Brother bother

'Come on, put your hands up!' the woman commanded. An evil grin spread across her face as she pointed the nozzle straight at my head.

I was in no position to argue with her. I put my hands up. She took aim and pressed. There was a hiss, then a cloud of spray as my hands were covered in a sickly, sweet-smelling scent.

I was in the perfume department of Dobbins department store. A saleswoman with black hair, long lilac fingernails and teeth

like tombstones was trying to sell me a bottle of scent.

'I don't want any!' I told her.

'Don't you care for the delightful fragrance of summer roses?' she simpered.

'Yes,' I replied. 'But what you've sprayed on my hands smells more like the stuff my mum squirts down the toilet.'

The saleswoman looked up. 'Perhaps your girlfriend would like to try a little? If she likes it, you could buy her a bottle for Christmas.'

'I haven't got a girlfriend!' I spluttered.

'Hi, Charlie!' called a cheery voice behind me. I turned round and saw M.

'She's not my girlfriend,' I told the saleswoman. 'She's my mechanic.'

She was also the reason I was in Dobbins' perfume department. I'd arranged to meet M there with her little brother, Troy. We were going to take him to see Father Christmas. As it was raining outside, I thought I'd wait inside.

A word about M's little brother, Troy: pest. Another word about M's little brother, Troy: monster. This was why M had asked me to come along; when Troy's around, there's always trouble and you're likely to need The Wheels for a quick getaway.

We got to the entrance to the grotto, only to find a big, burly security guard barring our way.

'You can't go in there,' he snarled.

I can't say I was surprised. No doubt he recognized Troy from last year, when Father Christmas had given him a bow and arrow. Never mind that it was just a toy one with little rubber pads at the end of the arrows – Troy had proceeded to shoot three of Santa's reindeer.

Then I realized that the security guard wasn't just talking to us, but to everybody who was queuing up to go into the grotto.

'Wanna see Santa!' wailed Troy. That got all the other little kids going, 'Wanna see Santa! Wanna see Santa!'

'Well, you can't!' growled the security guard.

'Why not?' snapped one of the mums.

'Because,' the security guard snapped back, 'he's done a runner. And he's taken all the presents with him. You'd better believe it, lady, Father Christmas is a villain and a thief!'

Chapter 2

A surprise visit

We all stood there, open-mouthed, hardly able to believe what the security guard had just told us. Even the little kids were quiet – but not for long.

Suddenly, the silence was broken by the distant sound of approaching police cars. Now, led by Troy, the kids all started screaming, 'Wanna see the police cars! Wanna see the police cars!'

Troy yanked M's hand, M yanked my hand and off we went.

Outside, the police were busy taking statements from the shop staff. Up in the sky, a police helicopter hovered menacingly. There was no doubt about it – if Father Christmas was hoping to make his getaway over the rooftops in his sleigh, he wasn't going to get very far.

'Look,' said M. 'I'll take Troy back to Mum's. Then I'll come round to your place.'

'Good plan,' I said. 'I'm sure, between us, we can solve this cruel and calculating Father Christmas crime!'

When I got in, I went through to the kitchen. Tracking down a thieving Father Christmas was likely to be a long and arduous task and I needed to make sure I had a decent meal inside me. I made myself a banana and tomato ketchup sandwich, and switched on the radio.

There was a local news item about the Santa scandal:

'Police have issued a description of the man they want to interview in connection with the theft of a sack of toys from Santa's grotto at Dobbins department store. He is jolly and plump, with a thick white beard and is wearing a bright red jacket with little white furry cuffs.'

That would make finding Father Christmas easier, I thought. At least now we had a description of the person we were looking for.

Suddenly, there was a furious knocking on the back door.

'Come in!' I called. 'It's open.'

I looked up, expecting to see the familiar figure of M. Instead, I saw a jolly and plump man with a thick white beard, wearing a bright red jacket with little white furry cuffs.

'Aaaargh! Father Christmas!' I screeched in a high-pitched squeal.

'Sssh, keep your voice down!' snapped Father Christmas.

'Aaaargh! Father Christmas!' I repeated in a deep-down, low voice.

In one swift movement, I swung The Wheels round so that I was between Father Christmas and the door. I gave him a long, hard stare.

'So, you thought you could fool Charlie, Prince of Wheels, by coming in the back door instead of down the chimney, did you?'

Father Christmas frowned. 'Were you expecting me?'

'Yes! I mean er ... no. I mean, as I'm half of Puddlethorpe-on-Sea's Toppermost Detective Duo, I was of course expecting to catch you sooner or later – only perhaps not quite so soon as this. Still, as you're here I might as well call the police. Then they can come round and arrest you and lock you up for a very, very long time indeed!'

I took out my phone. As I began to dial, a hand suddenly appeared over my shoulder and snatched the phone from me. I turned round and found myself facing a pair of very determined looking elves.

'I wouldn't do that if I were you,' said the elf who was holding my phone.

'Neither would I,' said the other elf.

'And for one very good reason,' said the first elf.

'And what's that?' I asked.

'Father Christmas is not guilty!' exclaimed the first elf.

'Father Christmas is innocent,' declared the second elf.

'And not only that, I never did it!' snapped Father Christmas angrily.

Then the two elves pulled off their pointy little hats and, with a gasp, I recognized their true identities.

Chapter 3

The whole story

'Rusty!' I said to the elf who had snatched my phone. 'Dusty!' I said to the other one.

The elf with the phone shook her head. 'No, bozo! I'm Dusty. She's Rusty.'

'Whatever,' I said. 'You can't deny that you're Rusty and Dusty, the Binns twins from my class at school.' The Binns twins were famous for two things: one, they were identical twins; two, they looked exactly like each other.

Suddenly, Rusty flung her arms around Father Christmas. 'Oh, Dad,' she cried.

Then Dusty flung her arms around Father Christmas and she cried, 'Oh, Dad,' too.

I gasped. My private detective's brain told me that this could mean only one of two things: Father Christmas was disguised as Rusty and Dusty's dad, or Rusty and Dusty's dad was disguised as Father Christmas.

Just at that moment, M burst in.

'M!' chorused Rusty and Dusty together.

'Did you get our text?' asked Dusty.

M nodded. 'I think you'd better sit down and tell me and Charlie the whole story from beginning to end,' she said.

'What, even including the really long, boring bit in the middle?' asked Rusty.

'No, leave out the long, boring bit in the middle,' I advised.

M, Rusty, Dusty, Father Christmas and I all sat around the kitchen table.

'It's like this,' Rusty began. 'Every year our dad works as Father Christmas at Dobbins. And every year we're his two elves. This morning, Dusty and I were about to leave for Dobbins when we got a text to say that Little Ben, who was football training with the Puddlethorpe Under 7s, wasn't well and would we go and pick him up.'

I knew Little Ben well. He was Rusty's and Dusty's little brother and was not to be confused with Big Ben, which is a bell in a clock tower at the Houses of Parliament.

'Anyway,' Dusty went on, 'when we got to the playing fields, we found that Little Ben was fine. The text had been a hoax! Next thing we know, we got a call from Dad telling us all the toys have been nicked from the grotto and the police are after him! We told him he needed the help of a top detective in Puddlethorpe, somebody who would stop at nothing to see justice done.'

'And straight away, you thought of me,' I said with a smile.

'No,' Rusty replied. 'Straight away, we thought of ace detective Scott Landyard in the High Street, but he's gone skiing for Christmas.' She sighed, then turned and looked at me. 'So then we reckoned, well ... you'd be better than nothing.'

Suddenly, the kitchen was filled with the noise of what sounded like a giant earthquake. Then I realized it was only Dusty, blowing her nose. There were tears in her eyes as she said, 'Can you and M find the missing toys and prove that our dad is innocent?'

Chapter 4
Santa's not-so-little helpers

'We'll help you, Dusty,' replied M, reassuringly. 'No problem! Now, Mr Binns, can you describe this sack of toys for us?'

'It's, er ... like a sack, with, er ... TOYS written on it,' answered Mr Binns.

'There's another thing M and I need before we can make a start on this case,' I said.

'What's that?' asked Rusty.

'A clue,' I replied.

'I think I can help you there,' said Mr Binns. 'Do you know the flash new megastore that's just opened in Puddlethorpe?'

'Cheetham and Swindlems?' M asked.

'That's the place,' said Mr Binns. 'They want to put Dobbins out of business. I heard a rumour they were going to open their own Santa's grotto. What better way to make sure it does well than to get Dobbins' Santa's grotto closed?'

'But how did they get into your grotto and steal the toys?' I asked.

Mr Binns frowned and thought hard for a moment. 'I think your best chance of finding the answer to that question is to go and interview my two little helpers. They might have seen something.'

'I didn't think you had any helpers? Rusty and Dusty had been sent to the playing field by the hoax text,' I said.

Mr Binns nodded. 'That's right. In fact, I got a call to say they wouldn't be coming in.'

'But you still had two elves helping you?' M asked.

'Yes,' said Mr Binns. 'I just presumed that Mr Dobbins had sent them when he heard the girls weren't coming in.'

'What did these stand-in elves look like, Mr Binns?' I asked.

Mr Binns thought for a moment. 'One was mean-looking and tall and the other was mean-looking and short,' he answered.

I took a deep breath. Then I put it back again. 'There are only two people in Puddlethorpe who answer to that description,' I said.

M nodded, a serious look on her face.

'Who's that?' Dusty wanted to know.

'Have you ever heard of Ed Banger and Mo Mash, leaders of the dreaded Bangers and Mash gang?' I asked.

'No,' said Rusty, with a shrug. 'The only Ed Banger and Mo Mash that I know are two horrible boys in our class at school.'

'That's who I'm talking about!' I said.

'Wow! Are Ed Banger and Mo Mash a couple of criminal crooks?' Rusty asked.

I nodded. 'Not only that, they're a pair of villainous villains as well.'

Rusty and Dusty gasped.

'Come to think of it, they do get given a lot of lunchtime detentions,' said Dusty.

'You three had better stay here,' M told the twins and Mr Binns. 'Don't answer the door, and draw the curtains.'

I handed Rusty a sheet of paper and a pencil.

'What's that for, Charlie?' she asked.

'So you can draw the curtains,' I replied.

'Bozo!' muttered M.

'Right, M,' I said, firmly. 'It's time you and I took The Wheels for a spin.'

Chapter 5

Toy trap

M leapt onto the back of The Wheels and in no time at all we hit the mean streets of Puddlethorpe-on-Sea. Then I felt a thump on my nose. It could mean only one thing: the mean streets were hitting me back.

Since M had refined the aerodynamic styling on the front wheel arches, I was the fastest driver on six wheels. When I went round corners, I was the fastest driver on three wheels.

As we raced down the High Street, M called out, 'Cheetham and Swindlems is down the next side street – next to Fred's and Betty's Beds and Settees furniture shop!'

I screeched around the corner, slammed on the brakes and crashed into a NO PARKING sign.

'Awwwww!' I groaned. I felt like a piece of cod in the fish and chip shop, i.e. very, very battered.

I turned round. 'Are you all right, M?'

'Apart from the side of me that's all left,' M replied. She looked at The Wheels and shook her head sadly. 'You made a bit of a mess of the aerodynamic styling on the front wheel arches though.'

As we approached the doors to Cheetham and Swindlems, we saw a man standing in the entrance. He looked mean, he looked mad. And he looked very, very bad.

'I recognize that man! That's Sir Grisly Swindlem himself!' M whispered to me. 'I saw him on TV, boasting about how he was going to take over every shop in Puddlethorpe!'

eek!

'And he's the man Rusty and Dusty's dad reckons is behind the Dobbins Santa scam?'

'He's the one,' said M.

All of a sudden, Sir Grisly Swindlem saw us. His face twisted into an ugly kind of sneer that comes easily to people who suck lemons for a hobby.

'M!' I hissed.

'What?'

'Can we go home now?'

But Sir Grisly Swindlem was already standing in front of us.

'Hello nice little children!' he snarled. 'Have you come to see Santa?'

M and I nodded, too scared to speak.

'Go right through to the back of the store,' he cackled, his voice screeching like a rusty hinge.

M and I hurried into the shop. We joined the stream of parents and children heading for Santa's grotto. When we got there, we saw a sign that said FREE ENTRY!

'What do you make of that?' asked M.

'Perhaps Sir Grisly Swindlem is a good guy, after all?' I suggested.

M shook her head. 'I don't think so somehow,' she muttered. 'Look!'

There in front of us was Cheetham and Swindlems' Father Christmas. He was well over two metres tall.

'Incredible!' I muttered.

M shook her head. 'Inflatable,' she replied.

I saw that M was right. Cheetham and Swindlems' Father Christmas was one of those great big blow-up ones you put on your roof!

'Sir Grisly Swindlem is too mean to even pay for a real Father Christmas,' M said.

All around us, kids were screaming their heads off, terrified by the monster inflatable Father Christmas.

Suddenly, I heard a voice yell, 'Can't you get your horrible snotty kids to stop that racket?'

I turned and saw that the voice belonged to one of Santa's elves – an elf I recognized as none other than Ed Banger!

'Give my kid one of your toys and we'll go,' shouted one of the mums.

'OK, missus,' replied Ed Banger, taking a toy from a sack marked TOYS. 'That'll be twenty pounds!'

M gave me a nudge. 'They're Dobbins' toys, I'll bet!'

'Twenty pounds? This place is a rip off!' yelled another mum. 'Let us out of here!'

'Certainly!' laughed the elf also known as Ed Banger. 'That'll be another twenty pounds – each!'

'So that's what Sir Grisly Swindlem is doing!' exclaimed M. 'It's free to get into the grotto, but it's twenty pounds to get out!'

'Not only that,' I said, 'it's twenty pounds to buy a toy – toys which he's nicked from Dobbins!'

Even the inflatable Father Christmas was trying to escape and float away, but he was being kept in place by a length of string held by the other elf who was, of course, Mo Mash!

'Ed Banger! Mo Mash!' I yelled. 'You're nicked!'

Ed and Mo spun round and saw us.

'Oh no we're not!' Ed Banger chanted back.

'Oh yes you are!' I yelled.

'Charlie, you're not in a pantomime now!' M snapped.

'Oh yes I am,' I replied.

'Run for it, Mo!' shouted Ed Banger, charging out through the back of the grotto.

Then Mo let go of the inflatable Father Christmas and ran off after Ed.

Chapter 6

A smashing time

The giant inflatable Santa floated across the grotto towards The Wheels. It thumped gently into the aerodynamic styling on the offside front wheel arch which had been bent and twisted when I'd hit the NO PARKING sign outside the shop.

'Oo-er!' I mumbled.

There was the sound of steady, insistent hissing. The monster in front of me was no longer a giant inflatable Father Christmas; it was a giant *deflatable* Father Christmas.

All around us, little kids wept, wailed and watched in horror as Father Christmas flopped, flapped and fluttered into a crumpled heap on the floor.

'Just what is going on here?' boomed a terrible voice.

M and I both looked up and found ourselves peering into the mean and nasty face of Sir Grisly Swindlem himself.

'Swindlem!' I shouted. 'You won't get away with this!'

'Oh yes I will!' snarled Sir Grisly Swindlem, turning on his heel and running off into the store.

'Oh no you – '

'Charlie, just shut up and get after him!' M bawled into my ear as she leapt onto the back of The Wheels.

I opened the throttle. The tyres squealed as we raced after Sir Grisly.

'Can you see him?' M asked. 'Over there! He's running through that doorway which says CHINA THIS WAY.'

'But we can't go there!' I protested.

'Why not?' asked M.

'I don't speak Chinese!'

'Bozo!' M yelled.

We had a smashing time in the china department. In fact, we smashed sixty soup bowls, seventy saucers and eighty egg cups.

Down the ramp we raced, into the rugs and carpets department.

Suddenly, Sir Grisly Swindlem looked over his shoulder to see how much we were gaining on him.

'Aaaargh!' he yelled as he tripped over the edge of an enormous rug. He fell flat on his face. As we drew level with him, M stuck out her leg and kicked the edge of the rug. It started to roll itself up, with Sir Grisly Swindlem inside it.

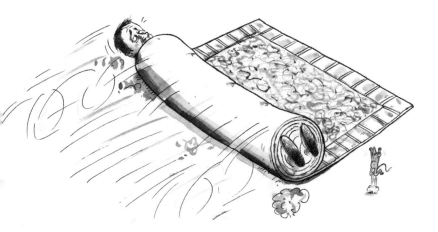

It rolled all the way across the floor and then hit a stack of carpets, which came crashing down on top of the rug – and Sir Grisly Swindlem.

'Aww …' moaned Sir Grisly Swindlem dizzily.

He stuck one hand out, then another.

'What a pity we haven't got a pair of handcuffs,' I muttered.

M handed me a pair of handcuffs.

'Thanks M,' I said, putting the handcuffs on Sir Grisly. 'What! How? I mean … where did you get these?'

'Troy nicked them from the police officer outside Dobbins,' she explained. 'I was going to take them back to the station, but I er … forgot.'

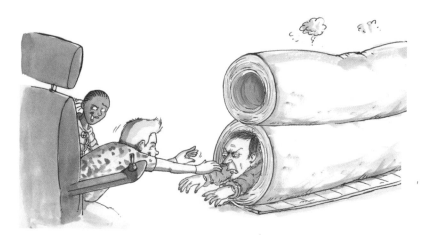

The police came and, once they heard our story, they took Sir Grisly Swindlem away. Mr Binns, Rusty and Dusty all got their jobs back and Dobbins department store had more visitors to its Santa's grotto than ever before. Ed and Mo went to court and the magistrate gave them both a very long sentence. And this was the sentence:

'In the whole of my one hundred and twenty-five years as a magistrate in this court, I have never come across such a pair of heartless hoodlums as the two defendants you see standing here before me in this court today, who have been found guilty of the grievous crime of stealing a sack of toys from Mr F. Christmas of The Grotto, Dobbins department store, Puddlethorpe-on-Sea.'

All in all, I reckoned, it was another brilliant result for Puddlethorpe-on-Sea's Toppermost Private Detective Duo.

Chapter 7

Some you win . . .

A few days later, M and I went to Dipstick's Garage, where she busied herself hammering the offside front wheel arch back into shape.

'Thanks M,' I said, when she'd finished.

'That's all right,' replied M, taking off her protective helmet. 'Now you can do something for me.'

'Sure,' I shrugged.

'Well,' M said, 'now that Father Christmas is back at Dobbins, I promised Mum we'd take Troy – '

'Aaaargh!' I yelled. 'Nooooooooooo!'

'Oh, come on, Charlie,' smiled M. 'Don't be such a wimp!' She leapt onto the back of The Wheels.

As we motored along the mean streets of Puddlethorpe-on-Sea, she leant over and hissed in my ear, 'Oh, and while we're in Dobbins, you can buy me a bottle of that perfume you were testing out!'

I sighed. That's the way it is being half of the Toppermost Private Detective Duo in Puddlethorpe-on-Sea. Some you win and some ... M wins.

About the author

I live on the Sussex coast
with my wife and two sons. We have nine
sheep, seventeen chicken, five ducks, a dog
and a cat. When I was at school there were
two things I wanted to be – 1: a grown-up,
and 2: a great detective. Well, I achieved one
of those two ambitions!

As a boy, my favourite book was *Norman and
Henry Bones: the Boy Detectives*. I still enjoy
a good detective story. All detectives need to
get about quickly – Sherlock Holmes had his
hansom cabs, Norman and Henry Bones had
their bikes. Charlie is special though – he has
The Wheels.